Time for a Party

Contents

Waking up time

At 7 o'clock Anna woke up.

It was her birthday.

Breakfast time

At 8 o'clock Anna had breakfast with Mum and Dad. They talked about Anna's party.

Shopping time

At 9 o'clock Anna and Mum
went shopping.

They bought some food for the party.

Cooking time

At 11 o'clock Dad made the
birthday cake.

Anna and Mum made the rest of
the party food.

Decorating time

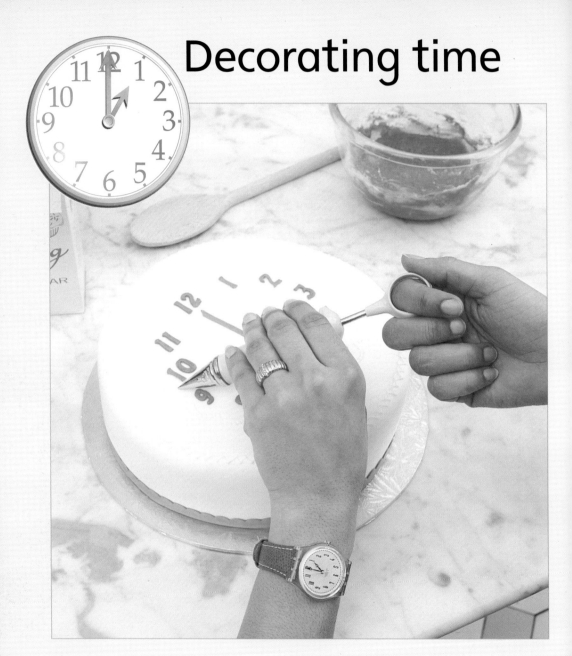

At 1 o'clock Mum decorated the birthday cake.

Anna and Dad decorated the house.

Party time

At 3 o'clock the party was ready.

All Anna's friends came.

They had a lot of fun.

Clearing up time

At 6 o'clock the party was over.

It was clearing up time.

Bedtime

At 7 o'clock Anna went to bed.

She was tired but happy.

Party timeline

7 o'clock

8 o'clock

9 o'clock

11 o'clock

1 o'clock

3 o'clock

6 o'clock

7 o'clock

Index

a
b
c
d
e
f
g
h
i
j
k
l
m
n
o
p
q
r
s
t
u
v
w
x
y
z